KT-873-327

Chicken Soup with Almonds

This soup can also be made using turkey or pheasant breasts. Pheasant gives a stronger, gamey flavour.

SERVES 4

1 large or 2 small boned and skinned chicken breasts
1 tbsp sunflower oil
1 carrot, cut into julienne strips
4 spring onions (scallions), thinly sliced diagonally
750 ml/1¼ pints/3 cups chicken stock
finely grated rind of ½ lemon
45 g/1½ oz/⅓ cup ground almonds
1 tbsp light soy sauce
1 tbsp lemon juice
30 g/1 oz/¼ cup flaked (slivered) almonds, toasted
salt and pepper

1 Cut each breast into 4 strips lengthways, then slice very thinly across the grain to give chicken shreds.

2 Heat the oil in the wok, swirling it around until really hot. Add the chicken and toss for 3–4 minutes until sealed and almost cooked through. Then add the carrot and continue to cook for 2–3 minutes, stirring all the time. Add the spring onions (scallions) and stir.

3 Add the stock to the wok and bring to the boil.

Add the lemon rind, ground almonds, soy sauce, lemon juice and plenty of seasoning. Bring back to the boil and simmer, uncovered, for 5 minutes, stirring occasionally.

4 Add most of the toasted flaked (slivered) almonds and continue to cook for a further 1–2 minutes. Season to taste.

5 Serve the soup very hot, in individual bowls, sprinkled with the remaining toasted almonds.

Fish & Vegetable Soup

This chunky fish soup flavoured with ginger and lemon makes a meal in itself.

SERVES 4

250 g/8 oz white fish fillets, such as cod, halibut, haddock, sole
½ tsp ground ginger • ½ tsp salt
1 small leek, trimmed and sliced
2–4 crab sticks (optional), defrosted if frozen
1 tbsp sunflower oil • 1 large carrot, cut into julienne strips
8 canned water chestnuts, sliced thinly
1.25 litres/2¼ pints/5 cups fish or vegetable stock
1 tbsp lemon juice • 1 tbsp light soy sauce
1 large courgette (zucchini), cut into julienne strips • pepper

1 Remove any skin from the fish and cut the fish into cubes, about 2.5 cm/ 1 inch. Combine the ground ginger and salt and rub into the fish. Leave to marinate for at least 30 minutes.

2 Meanwhile, divide the green and white parts of the leek. Cut each part into 2.5 cm/1 inch lengths and then into julienne strips, keeping the two parts separate. Slice the crab sticks into 1 cm/½ inch pieces.

3 Heat the oil in the wok, swirling it around so it is really hot. Add the white part of the leek and stir-fry for 2 minutes, then add the carrots and water chestnuts and cook for 1–2 minutes more, stirring thoroughly. Add the stock and bring to the boil, then add the lemon juice and soy sauce and simmer for 2 minutes.

4 Add the fish and continue to cook for about 5 minutes until the fish begins to break up a little, then add the green part of the leek and the courgettes (zucchini) and simmer for about 1 minute. Add the sliced crab sticks, if using, and season to taste with pepper. Simmer for 1–2 minutes and serve piping hot.

Prawn (Shrimp) Soup

**A mixture of textures and flavours
make this an interesting and colourful
soup. The egg may be made into a flat
omelette and added as thin strips.**

SERVES 4

2 tbsp sunflower oil
2 spring onions (scallions), sliced thinly diagonally
1 carrot, grated coarsely
125 g/4 oz large closed cup mushrooms, sliced thinly
1 litre/1³⁄₄ pints/4 cups fish or vegetable stock
½ tsp Chinese five-spice powder
1 tbsp light soy sauce
*125 g/4 oz large peeled prawns (shrimp) or peeled tiger
prawns (shrimp), defrosted if frozen*
½ bunch of watercress, trimmed and chopped roughly
1 egg, beaten well • salt and pepper
4 large prawns (shrimp) in shells, to garnish (optional)

1 Heat the oil in a wok, swirling it around until really hot. Add the spring onions (scallions) and stir-fry for 1 minute then add the carrots and mushrooms and continue to cook for about 2 minutes.

2 Add the stock and bring to the boil then season to taste with salt and pepper, five-spice powder and soy sauce. Simmer for 5 minutes.

3 If the prawns (shrimp) are really large, cut them in half before adding to the wok, then continue to simmer for 3–4 minutes.

4 Add the watercress to the wok and mix well, then slowly pour in the beaten egg in a circular movement so that it cooks in threads in the soup.

5 Adjust the seasoning and serve each portion topped with a whole prawn (shrimp).

Spinach & Tofu Soup

**Tofu (bean curd) is very popular
with vegetarians, being a good
source of protein.**

SERVES 4

*125–175 g/ 4–6 oz fresh spinach leaves,
or frozen leaf spinach, defrosted
small bunch of chives • 2 tbsp sesame oil
1 garlic clove, crushed
125–175 g/ 4–6 oz tofu (bean curd),
cut into 1 cm/ ½ inch cubes
60 g/ 2 oz/ ½ cup pine kernels
1 litre/ 1¾ pints/ 4 cups chicken or vegetable stock
½ tsp turmeric • ½ tsp ground coriander
2 tsp cornflour (cornstarch) • salt and pepper*

1 Rinse the spinach
thoroughly and remove
the stalks. Dry on paper
towels, then slice into thin
strips. If using frozen
spinach, drain well, then slice
or chop roughly.

2 Take 12 chives and tie 3
at a time into a knot to
use for a garnish, if liked.
Chop the remainder.

3 Heat the oil in a wok,
swirling it around until
really hot. Add the garlic and
tofu and stir-fry for 2–3
minutes until they are
beginning to colour. Add the
pine kernels and continue to
cook until they turn a light
golden brown. Add the stock,
turmeric, coriander and
seasoning and bring to the
boil; simmer for 10 minutes.

4 Blend the cornflour
(cornstarch) with a little
cold water and stir into the
wok. Add the strips of
spinach and simmer for a
further 2–3 minutes, stirring
frequently.

5 Adjust the seasoning, stir
in the snipped chives and
garnish each serving with a
chive knot, if liked.

Prawns (Shrimp) in Sauce

**Use raw tiger prawns (shrimp) with the
shell removed and just the tail left in place.**

SERVES 4

20–24 large raw tiger prawns (shrimp)
45 g/ 1½ oz/ ½ cup desiccated (shredded) coconut
90 g/ 3 oz/ 1¼ cups fresh white breadcrumbs
1 egg, beaten
600 ml/ 1 pint/ 2½ cups sunflower or vegetable oil
½ small honeydew or Ogen melon
fresh sprigs of coriander, to garnish

Peanut & coconut sauce:
60 g/ 2 oz creamed coconut
150 ml/ ¼ pint/ ⅔ cup hot water
125 g/ 4 oz crunchy peanut butter
2 spring onions (scallions), trimmed and finely chopped
1 tbsp dark soy sauce • 1 tsp brown sugar
2 tsp sesame seeds • salt and pepper

1 Peel the tiger prawns (shrimp), leaving the tails, and dry on paper towels. Put the coconut and breadcrumbs into a food processor and process until finely blended and chopped. Spread on a plate. Dip the prawns (shrimp) in the beaten egg, then coat in the coconut and breadcrumb mixture. Chill while making the sauce.

2 For the sauce, put the creamed coconut and water into the wok and blend thoroughly, then bring slowly to the boil. Remove from the heat, stir in the peanut butter, spring onions (scallions), soy sauce, sugar, sesame seeds and seasoning and when blended put into a serving bowl and keep warm.

3 Cut the melon into 12 slices, removing the seeds.

4 Wash and dry the wok, add the oil and heat to

180°–190°C/350°–375°F, or until a cube of bread browns in 30 seconds. Deep-fry the prawns (shrimp) a few at a time for 2–3 minutes until golden brown. Remove with a slotted spoon and drain on paper towels.

Keep warm while cooking the remainder.

5 Serve immediately on individual plates with slices of melon, garnished with sprigs of coriander. Serve the warm sauce separately.

Sole Paupiette

A delicate dish of sole fillets rolled up with spinach and prawns (shrimp), and served in a creamy ginger sauce.

SERVES 4

125 g/ 4 oz fresh young spinach leaves
2 Dover soles or large lemon soles or plaice, filleted
125 g/ 4 oz peeled prawns (shrimp), defrosted if frozen
2 tsp sunflower oil
2–4 spring onions (scallions), finely sliced diagonally
2 thin slices of ginger root, finely chopped
150 ml/ ¼ pint/ ⅔ cup fish stock or water
2 tsp cornflour (cornstarch) • *4 tbsp single (light) cream*
6 tbsp natural yogurt • *salt and pepper*
whole prawns (shrimp), to garnish (optional)

1 Strip the stalks off the spinach, rinse and dry on paper towels. Divide the spinach between the seasoned fish fillets, laying the leaves on the skin side. Divide half the prawns (shrimp) between them. Roll up the fillets from head to tail and secure with wooden cocktail sticks (toothpicks). Arrange on a plate in a bamboo steamer.

2 Stand a low metal trivet in the wok, add enough water to almost reach the top of it and bring to the boil. Place the bamboo steamer on the trivet, cover with the steamer lid and then the wok lid, or cover tightly with a domed piece of foil. Steam gently for 30 minutes until the fish is tender and cooked through. Remove the fish rolls and keep warm. Empty the wok and wipe dry.

3 Heat the oil in the wok, swirling it around until really hot. Add the spring onions (scallions) and ginger and stir-fry for 1–2 minutes. Add the stock and bring to the boil.

4 Blend the cornflour (cornstarch) with the

cream in a small bowl. Add the yogurt and remaining prawns (shrimp) to the wok and heat gently until boiling. Add a little sauce to the blended cream and add to the wok. Heat gently until thickened. Adjust the seasoning. Spoon the sauce over the paupiettes and garnish with whole prawns (shrimp), if liked.

Bajan Fish

Bajan seasoning comes from Barbados and can be used with all meat, fish, poultry and game. Add more chilli to make it really hot.

SERVES 4

500-625 g/ 1–1¼ lb monkfish tails, boned and cubed
2 large carrots • 175–250 g/ 6–8 oz baby sweetcorn cobs
3 tbsp sunflower oil
1 yellow (bell) pepper, cored, deseeded and thinly sliced
1 tbsp wine vinegar
150 ml/ ¼ pint/ ⅔ cup fish or vegetable stock
1 tbsp lemon juice • 2 tbsp sherry
1 tsp cornflour (cornstarch) • salt and pepper
fresh herbs and lemon slices, to garnish

Bajan seasoning:
1 small onion, quartered • 2 shallots
3–4 garlic cloves, crushed
4–6 large spring onions (scallions), sliced
small handful of fresh parsley • 2–3 sprigs of fresh thyme
small strip of green chilli pepper, deseeded,
or ½–¼ tsp chilli powder
½ tsp salt • ¼ tsp freshly ground black pepper
2 tbsp brown rum or red wine vinegar

1 First make the Bajan seasoning. Place all the ingredients in a food processor and process very finely.

2 Spread the Bajan seasoning in a shallow dish and press the fish into the seasoning, turning to coat evenly. Cover with cling film (plastic wrap) and leave to marinate in the refrigerator for at least 30 minutes, preferably overnight.

3 Cut the carrots into narrow 4 cm/1½ inch slices and slice the baby sweetcorn cobs diagonally.

4 Heat 2 tablespoons of oil in the wok, swirling it around until really hot. Add the fish and stir-fry for 3–4 minutes until cooked through. Transfer to a bowl and keep warm.

5 Add the remaining oil to the wok and when hot stir-fry the carrots and corn for 2 minutes, then add the (bell) pepper and stir-fry for 1–2 minutes. Return the fish and juices to the wok and stir-fry for 1–2 minutes.

6 Blend the vinegar, stock, lemon juice, sherry and seasoning with the cornflour (cornstarch). Stir into the wok and boil until the sauce thickens. Serve garnished with herbs and lemon slices.

Spiced Scallops

If using frozen scallops, make sure they are completely defrosted before cooking.

SERVES 4

12 large scallops with coral attached or 350 g/12 oz small
scallops without coral, defrosted if frozen
4 tbsp sunflower oil
4–6 spring onions (scallions), sliced thinly diagonally
1 garlic clove, crushed
2.5 cm/1 inch piece of ginger root, chopped finely
250 g/8 oz mangetout (snow peas)
125 g/4 oz button or closed cup mushrooms, sliced
2 tbsp sherry • 2 tbsp soy sauce
1 tbsp clear honey • ¼ tsp ground allspice
1 tbsp sesame seeds, toasted • salt and pepper

1 Rinse and dry the scallops, discarding any black pieces. Detach the corals, if using. Slice each scallop into 3–4 pieces and halve the corals if large.

2 Heat 2 tablespoons of oil in the wok, swirling it around until really hot. Add the spring onions (scallions), garlic and ginger, and stir-fry for 1–2 minutes. Add the mangetout (snow peas) and continue to stir-fry for 2–3 minutes. Transfer to a bowl.

3 Add the remaining oil to the wok. When really hot add the scallops and corals, and stir-fry for 2 minutes. Add the mushrooms and cook for 1–2 minutes.

4 Add the sherry, soy sauce, honey, allspice and salt and pepper to taste. Mix thoroughly, then return the vegetable mixture to the wok.

5 Season well and toss together over a high heat for 1–2 minutes until piping hot. Serve immediately, sprinkled with sesame seeds.

Fish with Saffron Sauce

**White steamed fish is served with a light
creamy saffron sauce with a real bite to it.**

SERVES 4

*625–750 g/ 1¼ – 1½ lb white fish fillets
(cod, haddock, whiting etc.)*
pinch of Chinese five-spice powder • 4 sprigs of fresh thyme
large pinch of saffron threads
250 ml/ 8 fl oz/ 1 cup boiling fish or vegetable stock
2 tbsp sunflower oil
125 g/ 4 oz button mushrooms, thinly sliced
grated rind of ½ lemon • 1 tbsp lemon juice
½ tsp freshly chopped thyme or ¼ tsp dried thyme
½ bunch watercress, chopped • 1½ tsp cornflour (cornstarch)
3 tbsp single (light) or double (heavy) cream • salt and pepper
lemon wedges and watercress sprigs, to garnish

1 Skin the fish and cut into 4 even-sized portions. Season with salt and pepper and five-spice powder. Arrange the fish on a plate and place in the bottom of a bamboo steamer, laying a sprig of thyme on each piece of fish (if the fillets are large you may need 2 steamers, one on top of the other).

2 Stand a low metal trivet in a wok and add water to almost reach the top of it. Bring to the boil, stand the bamboo steamer on the trivet and cover with the bamboo

lid and then the wok lid, or a domed piece of foil. Simmer for 20 minutes or until the fish is tender, adding more boiling water to the wok as necessary.

3 Meanwhile, soak the saffron threads in the boiling stock.

4 When the fish is tender, remove and keep warm. Empty the wok and wipe dry. Heat the oil in the wok, add the mushrooms and stir-fry for about 2 minutes. Add the saffron stock, lemon rind and

juice and chopped thyme and bring to the boil. Add the watercress and simmer for a 1–2 minutes.

5 Blend the cornflour (cornstarch) with the cream, add a little of the sauce from the wok, mix well, return to the wok and heat gently until thickened. Pour the sauce over the fish and serve, garnished with lemon wedges and watercress.

Sesame Salmon & Cream Sauce

Salmon fillets hold their shape when tossed in sesame seeds and stir-fried.

SERVES 4

625–750 g/ 1¼–1½ lb salmon or pink trout fillets
2 tbsp light soy sauce • 3 tbsp sesame seeds
3 tbsp sunflower oil
4 spring onions (scallions), thinly sliced diagonally
2 large courgettes (zucchini), diced,
or 12 cm/ 5 inch piece of cucumber, diced
grated rind of ½ lemon • 1 tbsp lemon juice
½ tsp turmeric • 6 tbsp fish stock or water
3 tbsp double (heavy) cream or fromage frais
salt and pepper • frisee (chicory), to garnish (optional)

1 Skin the salmon and cut into strips approximately 4 × 2.5 cm/ 1½ × 1 inches. Pat dry on paper towels. Season lightly, then brush with soy sauce and sprinkle all over with sesame seeds.

2 Heat 2 tablespoons of oil in the wok, swirling it around until really hot.

3 Add the salmon and stir-fry for 3–4 minutes until lightly browned all over. Remove with a fish slice, drain on paper towels and keep warm.

4 Add the remaining oil to the wok and when hot add the spring onions (scallions) and courgettes (zucchini) or cucumber and stir-fry for 1–2 minutes. Add the lemon rind and juice, turmeric, stock and seasoning and bring the mixture to the boil for 1 minute. Stir the cream or fromage frais into the sauce.

5 Return the salmon to the wok and toss gently in the sauce until really hot. Serve on warm plates and garnish with frisee (chicory), if using.

Chicken with Peanut Sauce

A tangy stir-fry with a strong peanut flavour. Serve with freshly boiled rice or noodles.

SERVES 4

4 boneless, skinned chicken breasts, about 625 g/1¼ lb
4 tbsp soy sauce • 4 tbsp sherry
3 tbsp crunchy peanut butter
350 g/12 oz courgettes (zucchini), trimmed
2 tbsp sunflower oil
4–6 spring onions (scallions), thinly sliced diagonally
1 × 250 g/8 oz can of bamboo shoots, drained and sliced
salt and pepper • 4 tbsp desiccated (shredded) coconut, toasted

1 Cut the chicken into thin strips across the grain and season lightly with salt and pepper.

2 Mix the soy sauce in a bowl with the sherry and peanut butter until smooth and well blended.

3 Cut the courgettes (zucchini) into 5 cm/ 2 inch lengths and then cut into sticks about 5 mm/ ¼ inch thick.

4 Heat the oil in the wok, swirling it around until it is really hot. Add the spring onions (scallions) and stir-fry for 1–2 minutes, then add the chicken and stir-fry for 3–4 minutes until well sealed and almost cooked.

5 Add the courgettes (zucchini) and bamboo shoots and continue to stir-fry for 1–2 minutes.

6 Add the peanut butter mixture and heat thoroughly, stirring all the time so everything is coated in the sauce as it thickens. Adjust the seasoning and serve very hot, sprinkled with toasted coconut.

Duck with Lime & Kiwi Fruit

Tender breast of duck served in thin slices with a sweet but very tangy sauce.

SERVES 4

4 boneless or part-boned duck breasts
2 large limes • 2 tbsp sunflower oil
4 spring onions (scallions), thinly sliced diagonally
125 g / 4 oz carrots, cut into matchsticks
6 tbsp dry white wine • 60 g / 2 oz / ⅓ cup sugar
2 kiwi fruit, peeled, halved and sliced • salt and pepper
parsley sprigs and lime halves, to garnish

1 Remove any excess fat from the duck breasts, then prick the skin all over with a fork or skewer and lay in a shallow dish in a single layer.

2 Remove the rind from the limes using a zester or grater and put into a bowl. Squeeze the juice from the limes (there should be 3 tablespoons or more; if not make up with lemon juice) and add to the bowl. Pour half the lime marinade over the duck breasts. Leave to stand in a cool place for at least 1 hour, turning at least once.

3 Drain the duck breasts. Heat 1 tablespoon of oil in the wok, swirling it around until really hot. Add the duck and fry quickly to seal all over. Lower the heat and cook for 5 minutes, turning several times until just cooked through and well browned. Remove and keep warm.

4 Wipe the wok clean with paper towels and heat the remaining oil in it. Add the spring onions (scallions) and carrots and stir-fry for about 1 minute then add the remaining lime marinade, wine and sugar. Bring to the boil and simmer for 2–3 minutes until slightly syrupy.

5 Add the duck breasts to the sauce, season well and add the kiwi fruit. Cook for about 1 minute until really hot and both the duck and kiwi fruit are well coated in the sauce.

6 Cut each duck breast into 'hinged' slices, open out into a fan shape and arrange on serving plates. Spoon the sauce over the duck, sprinkle with the remaining lime peel and garnish with parsley sprigs and lime halves.

Pork Balls with Minted Sauce

Made with lean minced pork, the balls are braised with stock and pickled walnuts to give a tangy flavour.

SERVES 4

500 g/ 1 lb lean minced pork
45 g/ 1½ oz/ ¾ cup fine fresh white breadcrumbs
½ tsp ground allspice • 1 garlic clove, crushed
2 tbsp freshly chopped mint
1 egg, beaten • 2 tbsp sunflower oil
1 red (bell) pepper, cored, deseeded and thinly sliced
250 ml/ 8 fl oz/ 1 cup chicken stock
4 pickled walnuts, sliced • salt and pepper
rice or Chinese noodles, to serve
fresh mint, to garnish

1 Combine the pork, breadcrumbs, seasoning, allspice, garlic and half the chopped mint in a bowl, then bind together with the egg. Dampen your hands and shape the meat mixture into 20 small balls.

2 Heat the oil in the wok, swirling it around until really hot, then stir-fry the pork balls until browned all over, about 4–5 minutes. Remove from the wok with a slotted spoon and drain thoroughly on paper towels.

3 Pour off all but 1 tablespoon of the fat and oil from the wok then add the red (bell) pepper and stir-fry for 2–3 minutes, or until softened, but not coloured. Add the stock and bring to the boil. Season well and add the pork balls, stirring to coat in the sauce; simmer for 7–10 minutes, turning occasionally. Add the remaining chopped mint and the pickled walnuts and continue to simmer for 2–3 minutes, turning the pork balls regularly to coat in the sauce.

4 Adjust the seasoning and serve with rice or Chinese noodles, or with a stir-fried vegetable dish, garnished with sprigs of fresh mint.

Red Spiced Beef

A spicy stir-fry flavoured with paprika, chilli and tomato, with a crisp bite to it from the celery strips.

SERVES 4

625 g/ 1¼ lb sirloin or rump steak • 2 tbsp paprika
2–3 tsp mild chilli powder • ½ tsp salt • 6 celery stalks
6 tbsp stock or water • 2 tbsp tomato purée (paste)
2 tbsp clear honey • 3 tbsp wine vinegar
1 tbsp Worcestershire sauce • 2 tbsp sunflower oil
4 spring onions (scallions), thinly sliced diagonally
4 tomatoes, peeled, deseeded and sliced
1–2 garlic cloves, crushed • Chinese noodles, to serve
celery leaves, to garnish (optional)

1 Cut the steak across the grain into narrow strips 1 cm/½ inch thick and place in a bowl. Combine the paprika, chilli powder and salt. Add to the beef and mix until the meat strips are evenly coated with the spices. Cover and leave to marinate for at least 30 minutes.

2 Cut the celery into 5 cm /2 inch lengths, then slice into strips about 5 mm/ ¼ inch thick.

3 Combine the stock, tomato purée (paste), honey, vinegar and Worcestershire sauce in a bowl.

4 Heat the oil in the wok, swirling it around until really hot. Add the spring onions (scallions), celery, tomatoes and garlic, and stir-fry for about 1 minute until the vegetables are beginning to soften. Then add the steak strips and stir-fry over a high heat for 3–4 minutes until the meat is well sealed.

5 Add the sauce to the wok and continue to stir-fry briskly until thoroughly coated and sizzling.

6 Serve with noodles and garnish with celery leaves, if using.

Sukiyaki Beef

**An easy way of giving beef a Japanese
flavour is to marinate it in teriyaki sauce
and sherry for anything from 1 to 24 hours.**

SERVES 4

2.5 cm/1 inch piece of ginger root, grated
1 garlic clove, crushed • 4 tbsp sherry • 4 tbsp teriyaki sauce
500–625 g/1–1¼ lb sirloin, rump or fillet steak
1 × 425 g/14 oz can of hearts of palm
2 tbsp sesame or sunflower oil
125 g/4 oz button or closed cup mushrooms, thinly sliced
salt and pepper

To garnish:
sesame seeds (optional) • spring onion (scallion) tassels

1 Blend the ginger in a shallow dish with the garlic, sherry and teriyaki sauce, adding a little salt.

2 Cut the steak across the grain into narrow strips about 2.5–4 cm/1–1½ inches long. Add to the marinade in the dish, mix thoroughly to coat, cover and leave in a cool place for 1–24 hours.

3 Drain the hearts of palm and cut into slanting slices about 1 cm/½ inch thick.

4 Remove the beef from the marinade with a slotted spoon, reserving the marinade. Heat the oil in the wok, swirling it around until really hot. Add the beef and stir-fry for 2 minutes, then add the mushrooms and continue to cook for 1 minute.

5 Add the hearts of palm to the wok with the reserved marinade and stir-fry for 1 minute, making sure the meat is evenly coated in the sauce. Adjust the seasoning, if necessary, and serve sprinkled with sesame seeds (if using) and garnished with spring onion (scallion) tassels.

Beef with Beans

Steak with a strong flavouring of sherry, teriyaki sauce and orange make an ideal dish for entertaining.

SERVES 4

500–625 g/1–1¼ lb sirloin, rump or fillet steak
1 orange • 2 tbsp sesame oil • 1 garlic clove, crushed
4 spring onions (scallions), thinly sliced diagonally
175 g/6 oz French (green) or fine beans, cut into 2–3 pieces
4 tbsp sherry • 1½ tbsp teriyaki sauce
1¼ tsp ground allspice • 1 tsp sugar
1 × 425 g/14 oz can of cannellini beans, drained
salt and pepper

To garnish:
orange slices • fresh bay leaves

1 Cut the steak into narrow strips, 4 cm/1½ inches long, cutting across the grain.

2 Remove the peel from the orange using a citrus zester, or pare thinly with a potato peeler, and cut the rind into julienne strips. Squeeze the orange and reserve the juice.

3 Heat 1 tablespoon of the oil in the wok, swirling it around until really hot. Add the strips of beef and stir-fry for 2 minutes, then remove from the wok and keep warm.

4 Add the remaining oil to the wok and when hot add the garlic and spring onions (scallions) and stir-fry for 1–2 minutes. Add the French (green) beans and cook for 2 minutes. Add the sherry, teriyaki sauce, orange rind and 3 tablespoons of orange juice, allspice, sugar and seasoning and when mixed return the beef and any juices to the wok. Stir-fry for 1–2 minutes then add the cannellini beans and stir until hot. Adjust the seasoning. Serve garnished with orange slices and bay leaves.

Five-Spice Lamb

Five-spice powder is a blend of ginger, cinnamon, fennel, star anise and cloves.

SERVES 4

625 g/1½ lb lean boneless lamb (leg or fillet)
2 tsp Chinese five-spice powder • 3 tbsp sunflower oil
1 red (bell) pepper, cored, deseeded and sliced thinly
1 green (bell) pepper, cored, deseeded and sliced thinly
1 yellow or orange (bell) pepper, cored, deseeded and sliced thinly
4–6 spring onions (scallions), sliced thinly diagonally
175 g/6 oz French (green) or fine beans,
cut into 4 cm/1½ inch lengths
2 tbsp soy sauce • 4 tbsp sherry
salt and pepper • Chinese noodles, to serve

To garnish:
strips of red and yellow (bell) pepper
fresh coriander (cilantro) leaves

1 Cut the lamb into narrow strips, about 4 cm/1½ inches long, across the grain. Place in a bowl, add the five-spice powder and ¼ teaspoon of salt, mix well and leave to marinate, covered, in a cool place for at least 1 hour and up to 24 hours.

2 Heat half the oil in the wok, swirling it around until really hot. Add the lamb and stir-fry briskly for 3–4 minutes until almost cooked. Remove from the wok.

3 Add the remaining oil to the wok and when hot add the (bell) peppers and spring onions (scallions). Stir-fry for 2–3 minutes, then add the beans and stir for 1 minute. Add the soy sauce and sherry and when hot add the lamb and any juices. Stir-fry for 1–2 minutes until the lamb is hot and coated in the sauce. Season and serve with noodles, garnished with strips of (bell) pepper and fresh coriander (cilantro).

Nasi Goreng

An Indonesian rice dish flavoured with vegetables, pork, soy sauce and curry spices.

SERVES 4

300 g/ 10 oz/ 1½ cups long-grain rice
350–500 g/ 12 oz–1 lb pork fillet or lean pork slices
3 tomatoes, peeled, quartered and deseeded
2 eggs • 4 tsp water • 3 tbsp sunflower oil
1 onion, thinly sliced • 1–2 garlic cloves, crushed
1 tsp medium or mild curry powder • ½ tsp ground coriander
¼ tsp medium chilli powder or 1 tsp bottled sweet chilli sauce
2 tbsp soy sauce • 125 g/ 4 oz frozen peas, defrosted
salt and pepper

1 Cook the rice in boiling salted water, following the instructions given in Chinese Fried Rice (see page 48) and keep warm.

2 Meanwhile, cut the pork into narrow strips across the grain, discarding any fat. Slice the tomatoes.

3 Beat each egg separately with 2 teaspoons of cold water and salt and pepper. Heat 2 teaspoons of oil in the wok, swirling it around until really hot. Pour in the first egg, swirl it around and cook undisturbed until set. Transfer to a plate and repeat with the second egg.

Cut the omelettes into strips about 1 cm/½ inch wide.

4 Heat the remaining oil in the wok and when really hot add the onion and garlic and stir-fry for 1–2 minutes. Add the pork and stir-fry for 3 minutes or until almost cooked. Add the curry powder, coriander, chilli powder or chilli sauce and soy sauce and cook for 1 minute, stirring constantly. Stir in the rice, tomatoes and peas and stir-fry for about 2 minutes until hot. Adjust the seasoning and turn into a heated serving dish. Arrange the strips of omelette on top and serve.

Rice with Crab & Mussels

**Mussels and crab add flavour and texture
to this spicy dish.**

SERVES 4, OR 6 AS A STARTER

300 g/ 10 oz/ 1½ cups long-grain rice
175 g/ 6 oz crab meat, fresh, canned or frozen
(defrosted if frozen), or 8 crab sticks, defrosted if frozen
2 tbsp sesame or sunflower oil
2.5 cm/ 1 inch piece of ginger root, grated
4 spring onions (scallions), thinly sliced diagonally
125 g/ 4 oz mangetout (snow peas), cut into 2–3 pieces
½ tsp turmeric • 1 tsp ground cumin
2 × 200 g/ 7 oz jars of mussels, well drained,
or 350 g/ 12 oz frozen mussels, defrosted
1 × 425 g/ 14 oz can of bean-sprouts, well drained
salt and pepper

To garnish:
crab claws or legs • 8 mangetout (snow peas), blanched

1 Cook the rice in boiling salted water, following the instructions given in Chinese Fried Rice (see page 48).

2 Extract the crab meat, if using fresh crab. Flake the crab meat or cut the crab sticks into 3 or 4 pieces.

3 Heat the oil in the wok, swirling it around until really hot. Add the ginger and spring onions (scallions) and stir-fry for 1 minute. Add the mangetout (snow peas) and cook for 1 minute. Sprinkle the turmeric, cumin and seasoning over the vegetables and mix well. Add the crab meat and mussels and stir-fry for 1 minute.

4 Stir in the cooked rice and bean-sprouts and stir-fry for 2 minutes or until hot and well mixed. Adjust the seasoning and serve very hot, garnished with crab claws and mangetout (snow peas).

Coconut Rice

A pale yellow rice flavoured with coconut and spices to serve as an accompaniment – or as a main dish with added diced meat.

SERVES 4

90 g/3 oz creamed coconut
750 ml/1¼ pints/3 cups boiling water
1 tbsp sunflower oil (or olive oil for a stronger flavour)
1 onion, thinly sliced or chopped
250 g/8 oz/1¼ cups long-grain rice • ¼ tsp turmeric
6 whole cloves • 1 cinnamon stick • ½ tsp salt
60–90 g/2–3 oz/½ cup raisins or sultanas (golden raisins)
60 g/2 oz/½ cup walnut or pecan halves, roughly chopped
2 tbsp pumpkin seeds (optional)
watercress sprigs, to garnish (optional)

1 Blend the creamed coconut with half the boiling water until smooth, then mix in the remainder and stir until well blended.

2 Heat the oil in the wok, add the onion and stir-fry gently for 3–4 minutes until the onion begins to soften but not brown.

3 Rinse the rice under cold running water, drain well and add to the wok with the turmeric. Cook for 1–2 minutes, stirring all the time. Add the coconut mixture, cloves, cinnamon stick and salt and bring to the boil. Cover with the wok lid, or a lid made of foil, and simmer very gently for 10 minutes.

4 Add the raisins, nuts and pumpkin seeds, if using, and mix well. Cover the wok again and cook for 5–8 minutes or until all the liquid has been absorbed and the rice is tender. Remove from the heat and leave to stand, still covered, for 5 minutes before serving. Remove the cinnamon stick. Serve garnished with watercress sprigs, if liked.

Fried Rice with Prawns (Shrimp)

Use either large peeled prawns (shrimp) or tiger prawns (shrimp) for this rice dish.

SERVES 4

300 g/ 10 oz/ 1½ cups long-grain rice • 2 eggs
4 tsp cold water • 3 tbsp sunflower oil
4 spring onions (scallions), thinly sliced diagonally
1 garlic clove, crushed
125 g/ 4 oz closed cup or button mushrooms, thinly sliced
2 tbsp oyster or anchovy sauce
1 × 200 g/ 7 oz can of water chestnuts, drained and sliced
250 g/ 8 oz peeled prawns (shrimp), defrosted if frozen
½ bunch of watercress, roughly chopped
salt and pepper

1 Cook the rice in boiling salted water, following the instructions given in Chinese Fried Rice (see page 48) and keep warm.

2 Beat each egg separately with 2 teaspoons of cold water and salt and pepper. Heat 2 teaspoons of oil in a wok, swirling it around until really hot. Pour in the first egg, swirl it around and leave to cook undisturbed until set. Remove to a plate or board and repeat with the second egg. Cut the omelettes into 2.5 cm/1 inch squares.

3 Heat the remaining oil in the wok and when really hot add the spring onions (scallions) and garlic and stir-fry for 1 minute. Add the mushrooms and cook for 2 minutes. Stir in the oyster or anchovy sauce and seasoning and add the water chestnuts and prawns (shrimp); stir-fry for 2 minutes.

4 Stir in the cooked rice and stir-fry for 1 minute, then add the watercress and omelette squares and stir-fry for 1–2 minutes until hot. Serve at once.

Chinese Fried Rice

It is essential to use cold, dry rice with separate grains to make this dish properly.

SERVES 4, OR 6 AS AN ACCOMPANIMENT

750 ml/ 1¼ pints/ 3 cups water • ½ tsp salt
300 g/ 10 oz/ 1½ cups long-grain rice
2 eggs • 4 tsp cold water • 3 tbsp sunflower oil
4 spring onions (scallions), sliced diagonally
1 red, green or yellow (bell) pepper, cored,
deseeded and thinly sliced
3–4 lean rashers of bacon, rinded and cut into strips
200 g/ 7 oz fresh bean-sprouts
125 g/ 4 oz frozen peas, defrosted
2 tbsp soy sauce (optional) • salt and pepper

1 Pour the water into the wok with the salt and bring to the boil. Rinse the rice in a sieve under cold water until the water runs clear, drain well and add to the boiling water. Stir well, then cover the wok tightly with the lid or a lid made of foil, and simmer gently for 12–13 minutes, (do not remove the lid during cooking). Remove the lid, give the rice a good stir and spread out on a large plate or baking (cookie) sheet to cool and dry.

2 Beat each egg separately with salt and pepper and 2 teaspoons of cold water. Heat 1 tablespoon of oil in the wok, swirling it around until hot. Pour in the first egg, swirl it around and leave to cook until set. Remove to a board or plate; repeat with the second egg. Cut the omelettes into thin slices.

3 Add the remaining oil to the wok and when really hot add the spring onions (scallions) and (bell) pepper and stir-fry for 1–2 minutes. Add the bacon and stir-fry for 1–2 minutes. Add the bean-sprouts and peas and toss together; stir in the soy sauce, if using.

4 Add the cooked rice and seasoning and stir-fry for 1–2 minutes, then add the strips of omelette and continue to stir for about 2 minutes or until the rice is piping hot. Serve at once.

Aviyal

This can be served with any type of food, and makes a good vegetarian main dish.

SERVES 4

250 g/8 oz/2 ⅔ cups desiccated (shredded) coconut
or 125 g/4 oz creamed coconut
300 ml/½ pint/1¼ cups boiling water • *2 tbsp sunflower oil*
30 g/1 oz piece of ginger root, grated
2 onions, finely chopped • *1 garlic clove, crushed*
2 tsp ground coriander • *1 tbsp garam masala*
1 tsp turmeric
2 green (bell) peppers, cored, deseeded and sliced in thin rings
1 red or yellow (bell) pepper, cored, deseeded and
sliced in thin rings
2 carrots, cut into julienne strips
1 green chilli pepper, cored, deseeded and sliced (optional)
125–175 g/4–6 oz French (green) or fine beans,
cut into 7 cm/3 inch lengths
175 g/6 oz green broccoli, divided into florets
3 tomatoes, peeled, quartered and deseeded • *salt and pepper*

1 Soak the coconut in the boiling water for 20 minutes, then process in a food processor until smooth. Alternatively, blend the creamed coconut with the boiling water until smooth.

2 Heat the oil in the wok, swirling it around until really hot. Add the ginger, onions and garlic and stir-fry for 2–3 minutes until they are beginning to colour lightly.

3 Add the coriander, garam masala and turmeric and stir-fry for a few minutes then add the (bell) peppers, carrots, chilli, beans, broccoli and tomatoes, reduce the heat and stir-fry for 4–5 minutes. Add the coconut purée and seasoning and bring to the boil. Stir-fry for 5–8 minutes, until tender but with a bite to the vegetables. Serve as a main dish with rice or noodles, or as a curry accompaniment.

Caraway Cabbage

This makes a delicious vegetable accompaniment to all types of food: it can also be served as a vegetarian main dish.

SERVES 4

500 g/ 1 lb white cabbage
1 tbsp sunflower oil
4 spring onions (scallions), thinly sliced diagonally
60 g/ 2 oz/ ½ cup raisins
60 g/ 2 oz/ ½ cup walnut pieces or
pecan nuts, roughly chopped
5 tbsp milk or vegetable stock
1 tbsp caraway seeds
1–2 tbsp freshly chopped mint
salt and pepper
sprigs of mint, to garnish

1 Remove any outer leaves from the cabbage and cut out the stem. Shred the leaves very finely, either by hand or using the fine slicing blade on a food processor.

2 Heat the oil in a wok, swirling it around until it is really hot. Add the spring onions (scallions) and stir-fry for 1–2 minutes.

3 Add the cabbage and stir-fry for 3–4 minutes, keeping the cabbage moving all the time by stirring from the outside to the centre of the wok. Make sure the cabbage does not go brown.

4 Add the raisins, walnuts and the milk or stock and stir-fry for 3–4 minutes or until the cabbage begins to soften slightly but is still crisp.

5 Season well, add the caraway seeds and 1 tablespoon of the chopped mint and stir-fry for 1–2 minutes. Serve sprinkled with the remaining chopped mint and garnish with sprigs of fresh mint.

Mixed Bean Stir-Fry

**Any type of canned beans can be used, but
rinse and drain well before use.**

SERVES 4

1 × 425 g / 14 oz can of red kidney beans
1 × 425 g / 14 oz can of cannellini beans
6 spring onions (scallions)
*1 × 200 g / 7 oz can of pineapple rings or pieces in
natural juice, chopped*
2 tbsp pineapple juice • 3–4 pieces stem ginger
2 tbsp ginger syrup from the jar
thinly pared rind of ½ lime or lemon, cut into julienne strips
2 tbsp lime or lemon juice • 2 tbsp soy sauce
1 tsp cornflour (cornstarch) • 1 tbsp sesame oil
*125 g / 4 oz French (green) beans,
cut into 4 cm / 1½ inch lengths*
1 × 250 g / 8 oz can of bamboo shoots, drained and sliced
salt and pepper • rice, to serve (optional)

1 Drain the beans, rinse under cold water and drain again thoroughly. Cut 4 spring onions (scallions) into narrow slanting slices. Thinly slice the remainder and reserve for garnish.

2 Combine the pineapple and juice, ginger and syrup, lime or lemon rind and juice, soy sauce and cornflour (cornstarch).

3 Heat the oil in the wok, swirling it around until really hot. Add the spring onions (scallions) and stir-fry for 1 minute. Add the French (green) beans and bamboo shoots and stir-fry for 2 minutes. Add the pineapple and ginger mixture and bring just to the boil. Add the canned beans and stir until very hot – about 1 minute.

4 Season to taste, and serve with boiled rice sprinkled with the reserved spring onions (scallions); or serve as a vegetable accompaniment.

Chinese Hot Salad

A mixture of vegetables stir-fried with a Chinese flavour, with an added touch of chilli. To serve cold, add 3–4 tablespoons of French dressing as the vegetables cool.

SERVES 4

1 tbsp dark soy sauce • 1½–2 tsp bottled sweet chilli sauce
2 tbsp sherry • 1 tbsp brown sugar • 1 tbsp wine vinegar
2 tbsp sunflower oil • 1 garlic clove, crushed
4 spring onions (scallions), thinly sliced diagonally
250 g/8 oz courgettes (zucchini), cut into julienne
strips about 4 cm/1½ inches long
250 g/8 oz carrots, cut into julienne strips
about 4 cm/1½ inches long
1 red or green (bell) pepper, cored, deseeded and thinly sliced
1 × 400 g/14 oz can of bean-sprouts, drained
125 g/4 oz French (green) or fine beans,
cut into 5 cm/2 inch lengths
1 tbsp sesame oil • salt and pepper
1–2 tsp sesame seeds, to garnish

1 Combine the soy sauce, chilli sauce, sherry, sugar, vinegar and salt and pepper to taste.

2 Heat the 2 tablespoons of sunflower oil in a wok, swirling it around until it is really hot. Add the garlic and spring onions (scallions) and stir-fry for 1–2 minutes. Add the courgettes (zucchini), carrots and (bell) peppers and stir-fry for 1–2 minutes, then add the soy sauce mixture and bring to the boil.

3 Add the bean-sprouts and French (green) beans and stir-fry for 1–2 minutes, making sure all the vegetables are coated with the sauce.

4 Drizzle the sesame oil over the vegetables, stir-fry for 30 seconds and serve sprinkled with sesame seeds.

Sweet & Sour Vegetables

Make your choice of vegetables from the suggested list, including spring onions (scallions) and garlic. For a hotter, spicier sauce add chilli sauce.

SERVES 4

5–6 vegetables from the following:
1 (bell) pepper, deseeded and sliced
125 g/4 oz French (green) beans, cut into 2–3 pieces
125 g/4 oz mangetout (snow peas), cut into 2–3 pieces
250 g/8 oz broccoli or cauliflower florets
250 g/8 oz courgettes (zucchini), cut into 5 cm/2 inch lengths
175 g/6 oz carrots, cut into julienne strips
125 g/4 oz baby sweetcorn cobs, sliced thinly
175 g/6 oz parsnip or celeriac, diced finely
13 celery sticks, sliced thinly crosswise
4 tomatoes, peeled, quartered and deseeded
125 g/4 oz button mushrooms, sliced
7 cm/3 inch length of cucumber, diced
200 g/7 oz can of water chestnuts or bamboo shoots, drained and sliced
425 g/14 oz can of bean-sprouts, drained
4 spring onions (scallions) sliced thinly
2 tbsp sunflower oil • 1 garlic clove, crushed

Sweet & sour sauce:
2 tbsp wine vinegar
2 tbsp clear honey • 1 tbsp tomato purée (paste)
2 tbsp soy sauce • 2 tbsp sherry
1–2 tsp sweet chilli sauce (optional)
2 tsp cornflour (cornstarch)

1 Prepare the selected vegetables, cutting them into uniform lengths.

2 Combine the sauce ingredients in a bowl, blending well together.

3 Heat the oil in the wok, swirling it around until really hot. Add the spring onions (scallions) and garlic and stir-fry for 1 minute.

4 Add the vegetables – the harder and firmer ones first – and stir-fry for 2 minutes. Then add the softer ones such as mushrooms, mangetout (snow peas) and tomatoes and continue to stir-fry for 2 minutes. Add the sweet and sour sauce to the wok. Bring to the boil quickly, tossing until the vegetables are thoroughly coated and the sauce has thickened. Serve hot.

Index